The Brook Hill Horses

CJ Race Horse With A Broken Leg

By

LISA DAWSON MACKEY

Illustrated By

MORGAN ROGERS

authorHOUSE®

AuthorHouse™
1663 Liberty Drive
Bloomington, IN 47403
www.authorhouse.com
Phone: 1 (800) 839-8640

Published by AuthorHouse   01/06/2017

ISBN: 978-1-5246-4831-2 (sc)
ISBN: 978-1-5246-4832-9 (e)

Print information available on the last page.

Any people depicted in stock imagery provided by Thinkstock are models, and such images are being used for illustrative purposes only. Certain stock imagery © Thinkstock.

This book is printed on acid-free paper.

Because of the dynamic nature of the Internet, any web addresses or links contained in this book may have changed since publication and may no longer be valid. The views expressed in this work are solely those of the author and do not necessarily reflect the views of the publisher, and the publisher hereby disclaims any responsibility for them.

Contents

Foreword

B rook Hill Farm is located in a picturesque setting at the foot of the Blue Ridge Mountains in Goode, VA. Horses that have been injured or cannot meet their owner's needs are donated to the farm. Most of the horses have been high level performance horses that have suffered career ending injuries. Due to the injuries, the horses are either no longer wanted by their owners, or their owners can no longer take care of them. If the horses were sold at auction, they would probably be sold for slaughter. Some horses come because the owners can do longer afford to feed them. Brook Hill Farm is a non profit organization that is dedicated to the rescue and rehabilitation of these horses and the preventing the slaughter of them. By combining the efforts of professionals and volunteers, most of these horses are able to resume healthy lives. Once a horse is declared healthy and sound, it is either placed, at no cost, in an adoptive home that meets the requirements set by Brook Hill's board of directors, or is used in the United Neigh program. Many of the horses are placed with United States Pony Club or 4-H members and go on to compete in horse and pony shows. Brook Hill continues to follow each animal after adoption to ensure them a lifetime of love and care. Brook Hill Farm has helped over 300 horses, and horses continue to arrive weekly.

It takes many hours of hard work to manage this farm and care for all these horses. I would like to thank Joanne Miller and all the professionals and volunteers who work so hard to make Brook Hill Farm a success; however, the continued successs relies on continued support. Therefore, I pledge to donate to Brook Hill Farm fifty percent of the profit of this book to support the work and programs at Brook Hill Farm. If you would like more information about Brook Hill Farm, the United Neigh program, or would like to join with me and support this wonderful program, please contact Brook Hill Farm online at www. BrookHillFarm.org

This book is a fictional retelling of the story of one of the horses which came to Brook Hill Farm. This story is based on a real horse, events, and people, but some of the names and details have been changed. This book is about one horse, CJ. However, many other people and horses were involved in the program and horse shows depicted in this book. In addition, many events depicted in this book were team events and all members of the team were important to the success of the team. These horses and team members may be elaborated on in future books or on the Brook Hill Farm web site. The cover pictures of this book are of the actual horse and his adoptive owner.

Chapter 1

The Arrival

One windy autumn day, Jo heard the sound of someone pulling down the long gravel drive at Brook Hill Farm. Joanne Miller, the owner of the farm, wasn't expecting any visitors on this day so wondering who was arriving, Jo grabbed her coat and headed out the back door. Equally curious, Samantha, Jo's ten year old daughter, looked out her second floor bedroom window and saw a white dual wheel truck towing a two horse trailer pulling toward the barn. By the long black tail hanging out the back of the trailer, "Sam" could tell a horse was in the trailer and was anxious to see the new arrival. She quickly put on her boots and ran downstairs just in time to catch the screen door as Jo went outside.

As Kate, the brown and white beagle, barked loudly, a tall, thin lady wearing tan riding pants and black English riding boots, stepped out of the pick up truck.

"Hello. I am Joanne Miller. Can I help you?" asked Jo as Sam stood by her side. Sam looked like a little version of Jo. Both were small with sandy brown shoulder length hair, brown eyes, and round faces.

The lady smiled at the two similar friendly faces looking at her, but appeared worried and sad as she introduced herself to Jo and Sam. "I have come a long way and have made several stops at places similar to this looking for a home for my horse," replied the lady. "But, I have been turned down by all of them," she stated in a weary voice.

She went on to tell the story of the horse on her trailer. The horse was named Curious Jorge, which she pronounced like Curious George, the monkey in the popular children's book. She called him CJ for short. He had been a race horse. Like most race horses, he started racing when he was two years old. She said he was very fast and won a lot but racing is hard on a horse's legs. One day when CJ was about three years old, as he was about to cross the finish line, he stumbled. His front legs rolled over his hoofs, breaking both fetlocks. This would be like breaking both of your ankles. He was carried off the track in a trailer and taken back to the owner's farm where he underwent an operation; however, after the operation, CJ was still lame. He could not walk without limping. He would never be able to race again. His days as a race horse were over and the owner did not want him any more. The owner put him in an auction. Lame horses do not sell well in auctions. Often, no one wants a lame horse and they sell to companies for meat. However, sometimes an ex-race horse can make a great show horse if it can become sound, not lame. This lady knew that and thought CJ had a chance to recover. So she purchased him in hopes of getting him sound and making him into a show horse. She figured she could resell him and make a lot of money. Unfortunately, when she got him home, CJ did not recover. She could not ride him, show him, or sell him for lots of money. Now she didn't want him any more either but she didn't want him to sell to a meat packing plant. She loved him and felt sorry for him. She wanted him to have a good home where someone would look after him and take good care of him, but, she could not find anyone who would take a lame horse. She had gotten the same answer at every farm she had taken him to; Brook Hill Farm was her last hope, and the last chance for CJ.

Never being one to say that there is no hope for a horse to recover and fully believing that horses, like humans, deserve to be properly cared and not inhumanely slaughtered. Jo was somewhat skeptical that the story was true but the thought of the horse being sold for slaughter upset Jo terribly. "Let's take a look at him," replied Jo being appalled at the thought of the horse being killed.

The lady unlatched the rear trailer door and pushed it open. She lowered the ramp and, to Jo and Sam's amazement, off backed a beautiful, tall, 16.3 hand, dark bay gelding. The horse was fit and lean like a race horse but looked tired as if he had been in the trailer a long time. He hung his head and acted so calm Jo wondered if he had been drugged. He was quiet and easy to handle. He didn't act like a race horse. He wasn't prancing around or excited by the dog barking and horses running in the field. The lady led him around so Jo could see how he walked. Sam stroked his long black mane as Jo checked him out. Jo noticed that the inside of his lip had been tattooed. This is proof that he had been registered with the jockey club as a race horse. (The dots of the tattoo are visible in the daylight but the actual tattoo requires a black light to be seen.) Jo and Sam both liked the horse immediately. He was sweet and appeared to enjoy the attention.

It didn't take Jo long to make a decision, "If you can pull off his shoes, we will keep him. We may not be able to make him sound, but we offer retirement services for horses. Brook Hill is committed to allowing horses to live as people want to live out their days, loved and cared for even if they can't perform as they once did," Jo stated, lovingly stroking CJ's face.

Overjoyed, the lady handed over the lead rope to Sam and quickly pulled off CJ's shoes. Before anyone could say another word, the lady got back in her truck and left immediately.

As the dust blew up behind the the truck Sam smiled at Jo and said, "I guess she was afraid you would change your mind."

Jo laughed and three of them, Jo, Sam, and CJ, headed off to the pasture.

"Why did you have her pull off his shoes?" asked Sam.

"He needs time to rest. His bones and feet need to heal," replied Jo. Jo knew that it would take a great deal of conditioning and at least six months to a year for an injury like CJ's to heal. She was hoping for the best and always thinking positively.

"We will have the vet look at him tomorrow. I have a good feeling about this horse," said Jo.

"Me too," agreed Sam. She had been raised around horses and loved them. Sam had been riding for a number of years and was a talented young rider. The big race horse touched her heart and the thought of riding him excited her.

"I will help take care of him," Sam offered, eager to get started.

Jo laughed and patted Sam's head. Jo knew Sam would be excited about the horse. "Lets turn him out and let him rest in the sunshine today. You can get his stall ready and bring him in tonight," replied Jo.

After watching CJ limp slowly down through the pasture and blend in with the other horses, Sam ran off to the barn.

Chapter 2

Work Hard

Sam went to the barn and cleaned out a stall. The barn was old and needed a new coat of paint but it provided shelter from the cold and rain. Sam worked hard digging out the old smelly manure, loading it into a wheelbarrow and hauling it to the manure pile. The wheelbarrow looked big compared to Sam, but Sam was used to working hard around the barn and didn't mind the work. After the stall was cleaned out Sam piled up a load of new, clean sawdust in the wheelbarrow and wheeled it back into the stall. The stall looked good as new by the time Sam finished. Then she filled a five gallon blue bucket with fresh water. It took all her strength to lift the bucket and hang it in the stall high enough for CJ to drink out of and not get his legs hung in it. Sam couldn't wait for the day to pass. Every hour she asked if it was time to get CJ. Finally, as the sun began to set, Jo said "yes," and off Sam ran.

Sam climbed up on the gate to the field and let out a loud whistle. All the horses came running through the field. There were all kinds of horses at Brook Hill. There were fat yellow palominos, small gray Arabians with pretty petite heads, black and white spotted pintos, brown and white paints with long black manes, and beautiful shiny solid blacks, bays, and sorrels. Some were quarter horses, some were thoroughbreds, some were big and some were small. Sam watched as the horses approached but none were CJ. Sam started to panic as CJ was no where to be seen. She worried that the other horses may have hurt him. Sam opened the gate and the herd headed to the barn. Most of the herd had been there a long time and they all knew the daily routine and automatically went to their own stalls. After they went through the gate Sam ran into the pasture calling for CJ. As she looked frantically around, she saw CJ struggling to make it up the hill. She felt relieved but sorry for him because she knew he was in pain. He limped slowly toward her as she ran down the hill to greet him. She rubbed his forehead as she clipped the lead onto his halter. He stood still and did not try get away. She walked slowly beside him not to rush him or force him to walk faster on his hurting hooves. Soon he would learn to follow the others and go in by himself, but today Sam was happy to walk beside him and show him to his new home.

Sam led him to his stall and tied him so she could brush him. As she curried his body he nuzzled her. He had big, dark brown, curious eyes. His name fits, thought Sam, as CJ looked in her pockets and checked out her every move. "Looking for a treat, are you?"

As she filled his feed tub with grain all the other horses started to neigh. Sam helped Jo grain and hay the horses then went back to check on CJ. She rubbed his neck and talked to him like he was a person as he munched on his hay. After he ate, he laid down on the soft bedding and Sam sat down beside him. As the night fell and the barn grew dark, Sam laid her head on CJ's warm fur and fell off to sleep with her new best friend. Molly, the golden retriever, sat on the barn porch and kept watch through the night.

As the sun came up and the rooster crowed, Sam woke up in her room and realized that Jo had carried her back to her own bed. Without stopping for breakfast, Sam ran to the barn to check on CJ. She helped feed and as the horses ate she began cleaning the stalls. Then she heard the familiar voice of the local vet.

"Good morning Sam," Dr. Vaughn called out.

Dr. Vaughn, the veterinarian, volunteered his time at Brook Hill. He was a kind, older gentleman with a large bushy gray mustache. Sam liked Dr. Vaughn and was eager to show him the newest arrival.

"Look what we got in. A real race horse!" Sam said as she showed the doc the tattoo on CJ's lip.

"Yep, looks like the real deal. Now hold still sweet pea," Dr Vaughn said soothingly to CJ as he took x-rays of CJ's legs and feet. Sam laughed because Dr Vaughn called all the horses sweet pea as he worked on them. Then Dr Vaughn showed Sam how to move CJ's hooves to create better flexibility to improve his ability to walk. He told Sam the she would need to do this every day in order for CJ to get better. He also cautioned her not to over exercise him and said that it would be a long slow process.

So, every morning, Sam got up at 5:00 am so she could feed and walk CJ to stretch his legs before she went to school. She would pick up his feet and move his hooves just like Dr Vaughn showed her. Then she would put him in the pasture before running down the driveway to catch the school bus. After school she would rush home and go straight out to the pasture to get CJ. Jo thought this was wonderful. She didn't have to call Sam numerous times to wake her up or listen to the usual complaints in the morning about having to get up. Instead, it was replaced by Jo having to call Sam to come in from the barn at night and do her homework. But Jo only had to tell Sam once, "If your grades fall, you will not be allowed to go to the barn until your grades get better. School comes first."

Sam studied hard and was a good student. She wasn't going to let bad grades keep her from CJ.

Jo thought this new interest would be short lived. She figured that Sam would get tired of getting up early and doing all the hard work that it took to care for a horse and do her school work too. But Sam secretly dreamed of riding CJ, so all winter long, Sam got up early every day and put on her gloves and boots, tramped through the mud on rainy days, snow on snowy days, and the freezing cold on all the other grey winter days to make sure CJ was groomed and exercised. CJ was like an athlete in training. He needed to be fit and in good condition. The grooming kept his coat shiny and the exercising kept his muscles in shape and strengthened his legs. The moving of his hooves loosened his tendons. Sam knew if CJ stood in a stall all day he could get stiff and sore. She also knew that this was his only chance to be sound. A sound horse is not lame and can be ridden. Sam was determined that CJ was going to heal. Jo also worried that Sam was going to be disappointed because there was no certainty that CJ would heal and his legs would hold up to the stress and strain of riding.

On the pretty days Sam would lead CJ through the fields and around the riding ring. She also taught him how to lounge. To do this, Sam took a long nylon rope and hooked one end to CJ's halter while holding the rest of the rope in her hand. She let CJ walk a circle around her while, little by little, letting out the rope. CJ walked farther and farther away until he was making about a ten foot circle around Sam. The she would click with her tongue and CJ would trot around the circle. They could not do too much in one day or it would make his injury worse. Instead, they did a little more each day to strengthen his muscles. CJ wasn't limping any more and was showing signs of improvement. Sam was anxious to do more but showed great patience in taking it slow and making sure CJ was able to move on before asking him to do more.

The next step was to teach CJ to canter, run, on the lounge line. So one day, on their way into the riding ring, Sam picked up the long black lounge whip. It had a long braided string tied to the end of it which was used to snap at the horse's rear heels to make him canter. But when Sam picked up the whip, CJ jumped. CJ didn't want to walk any more. This was a new side of CJ that Sam hadn't seen before. He was no longer the calm quiet horse he had been up to this point. He was hard to lead. Sam held tight to lead rope to hang onto him. He began trotting and prancing around with his head up. Sam jerked on the lead to make him stop, but he was excited and nervous, and he refused to stand still.

Jo was working with another horse in the riding ring and saw how CJ was acting. Jo knew what the problem was and called out to Sam, "CJ is scared of the whip! Race horses are use to being hit with whips to make them go faster. You will have to teach him not to be afraid. Show him that you are not going to hurt him."

So Sam held the whip low and pulled on the lounge line for CJ to stand still. She calmly walked closer to CJ, but CJ backed away. He raised his head and snorted at her.

"Easy boy, I'm not going to hurt you," Sam said soothingly as she walked toward him.

Jo watched as Sam worked with CJ. Jo was worried because Sam was so small compared to CJ and Jo didn't know if CJ would step on Sam or try to pull away and Sam would not be able to hold onto him. But Sam wasn't scared. She was experienced and knew what she was doing. Sam also didn't think that CJ would hurt her.

It took several attempts for Sam to get the whip close to CJ. Then Sam rubbed the whip like a brush all over CJ's body until he stood quietly. "See silly, its OK," Sam told CJ. It took time and practice for CJ to walk and trot calmly on the lounge line while Sam held the whip. Sam did not want to ask him to canter right away because she was concerned that he would jump and run so hard and fast that he would re-injure himself. So Sam worked on getting CJ use to being lounged with the whip in her hand before she even moved the whip. After several days she finally shook the whip and asked CJ to canter around the circle. CJ galloped around the circle like a pro. Feeling good, CJ tossed his head and kicked up his heels so Sam pulled on the lounge line and asked him to return to a trot which he did. Sam was pleased that he listened and had made a lot of progress.

Unfortunately, the next day, CJ appeared to give a little on his left front hoof when he trotted. This was not a good sign. Sam's heart sank. She couldn't believe it. After all her hard work! Sam immediately stopped and walked him back to the barn. She was really upset that he was still showing signs of lameness. She tied CJ in his stall to cool down before letting him eat and drink. Sam sat down on the blanket box and threw the lead rope down and kicked the dust.

"What's wrong?" inquired Jo noting Sam's bad mood.

"CJ is lame," pouted Sam. Jo too felt Sam's disappointment.

Trying to be positive Jo said, "It's only been a few months. Don't give up on him yet. It is awfully cold today. Maybe he will be better by spring."

"I know, I know," replied Sam as she slid off the box and went back to brush CJ.

The next day Sam ran back to the barn praying that CJ would be OK. He seemed fine as she led him out so Sam cued him to trot. This day CJ didn't limp when he trotted. Hope sprang back into Sam's heart and a smile crossed her face. Sam let him canter around a little bit but didn't work him very long or hard. "Baby steps" Sam kept telling herself. "You're going to be OK," Sam whispered to CJ as she hugged his neck. CJ nuzzled her in return as if he was hugging her back.

It was a long cold winter, but as always, spring brings new beginnings. The grass was turning green again and the flowers were starting to bloom. Daffodils were lining the fence row. The baby birds were chirping and new baby ducks were on the pond. Spotted baby deer could be seen in the pasture with their mothers.

One warm spring day, Sam and Jo went out to bring in the herd. Sam whistled as she had done every day, but this day, there was something different. The herd came running as usual but a new horse led the way. Running at full speed, with his head up, was CJ. He looked like a horse winning a race. He did not limp or show any signs of pain. He outran all the horses in the field. Sam and Jo looked in amazement and smiled at each other.

"Look at that! Can you believe it!" Sam said excitedly.

"Good work," complimented Jo. Both Sam and Jo knew CJ had recovered. At last, Sam knew that she would soon ride the big bay race horse.

Chapter 3

Be A Good Sport

At last that wonderful day came when Sam could put the saddle on CJ. He was ready to be ridden. Jo was still a little anxious that CJ would be rowdy because he had not been ridden in so long and she was not sure how excitable an old race horse would be under saddle. Jo was hesitant to let Sam be the first to get on him, but Sam insisted that she was going to be the first one to ride him and Jo knew she deserved it after all her hard work. Sam was not afraid but Jo made her lounge CJ for a little bit before getting on to make sure all the friskiness was out of his system. He didn't seem bothered by the saddle and appeared ready and willing to be ridden. Anxious to get started, Sam gathered up the lounge line and threw the reins over CJ's head. But Sam was short and CJ was tall, so after several attempts to raise her leg high enough to reach the stirrup, Sam headed to the mounting block. CJ moved a little as Sam jumped up on the block and placed her foot in the stirrup. As Sam climbed on, CJ immediately started shaking his head and prancing around. CJ had been so calm while they were working with him on the ground but he began to act different after Sam began to ride. He shook his head and pulled at the reins. He didn't want to walk; he hopped a little and continued to act a little goofy and silly tossing his head and playfully moving around. This was a much more energetic side of CJ that Sam had never seen before.

Jo watched from the middle of the ring. Jo was concerned that CJ might try to buck and run. She didn't want Sam to get thrown off and hurt. But she kept quiet because she did not want Sam to know how nervous she was feeling.

It had been a long time since CJ had been ridden and he was feeling good. Sam wasn't bothered about his behavior and found it kind of funny. Sam knew to keep him as quiet as she could because running could hurt his legs. Besides, he needed to learn to walk and be calm; he was not a race horse any more.

Every day they would walk and trot in the ring to warm up. This was just to warm up his muscles and loosen his legs and tendons. Every day CJ would start out acting goofy, getting out his playfulness. This was his routine and it came to be expected. Soon, she left the riding ring and off through the woods she rode. CJ was not scared of the squirrels scurrying up the trees but stopped to look at the deer eating apples off the ground near the old apple tree. He didn't jump or act concerned when the deer saw him and ran away. Sam was pleased with how CJ was on the trails. It didn't take long before they were trotting and galloping through the fields. When it was clear that his legs were going to hold up and the lameness was not coming back, Sam began working him in the riding ring with the other riders, boys and girls, who come to Brook Hill Farm three times a week to participate in the United Neigh Program.

This program is part of the local 4-H riding program. Children would come to Brook Hill several times a week as a club to do chores around the barn. They cleaned stalls and tack, and they helped care for the horses by feeding, brushing, and exercising them. Jo and other volunteers would patiently watch over all the children, assign chores, and hold a club meeting. The children were happy to do their chores because the reward was getting assigned their own horse. Some of the children, mostly girls, who came to Brook Hill, had never ridden or owned a horse. So, this was a great treat. They learned to care for, ride, and even show their horse. They were often surprised to learn how much practice it took to learn to ride a horse correctly and even more practice to train one properly and be good enough to show.

Sam, too, was learning lots from working with CJ. Even though Sam had ridden for years, CJ was like training a young horse. He was much more challenging than riding an older broke horse which had been trained for showing or pleasure riding. Jo would not allow children who had never ridden or who were not experienced riders to ride a horse like CJ, but she knew Sam was a good rider and was ready to take on the task. CJ had never been trained to be a show horse. Show horses aren't allowed to run as fast as they can around the ring. Show horses have to be calm and under control. They are judged on their temperament and movement.

One sunny spring day, as Sam was riding in the ring with the other girls, she secretly dreamed of being in a horse show. She longed for the day that her name would be called out as the first place winner! All the girls were cantering their horses around the ring and Sam began to pass a few of the other horses when suddenly, Sam's daydream came to an abrupt end. CJ took off! It was like he had a huge burst of energy as he ran past the other horses. His head was up and his tail flew back in the wind as if he was "off to the races." Jo could hear the pounding of hooves and turned to see what was happening. As Jo observed both horse and rider fly by she held her breath and prayed that Sam would not fall off and get hurt. The other horses became excited too. Some of the other horses sped up too and the girls became scared and began to pull their horses down to a walk. A few girls got off their horses and held them as they watched CJ run. Other girls stopped their horses and rubbed their necks to calm them down. It was obvious that CJ was out of control. Sam's heart raced. The world look like a blur as they raced by. Sam took a deep seat, squeezed tight with her legs and jerked on the reins. CJ stretched his neck and chomped down on the bit making it hard for Sam to pull the reins and stop him. He continued to run. It took all of Sam's strength to pull him into a small tight circle to get him to slow down and stop him from running.

"Good job," yelled Jo as she breathed a sigh of relief. "Way to hang with him."

"That's the fastest I have ever seen any horse run," chimed in Sarah. "Were you scared?"

Sam just smiled and shook her head "no" as she caught her breath. She liked the thrill and the challenge. Sam was a true rider. The excitement was part of why she enjoyed riding. She was learning about CJ and it would also make her a better rider. The horse that had seemed so calm had come to life. Sam soon learned that this quirky behavior was part of CJ. He was fine while they were on the ground, but he got excited when they rode with the other horses. He was pushy and hard to hold. He liked being in the front of the other horses. This was what he knew, and Sam was going to have to teach him to act differently. Being the fastest horse in a pleasure class on the flat at a horse show was not going to win him first place.

Jo knew there was a lot of work ahead for Sam. Just like there had been months of ground work preparing him to be ridden, there would be months of training and practice to prepare CJ to be a show horse. He needed to get out of the race horse frame of mind and change into a show horse. He truly needed to become a pleasure to ride.

So Sam practiced nearly every day that summer. She put in more "seat" time riding than any other child at the barn. She was determined to make CJ into a show horse. After a year of ground work and riding practice, Jo felt Sam and CJ were ready to go to a horse show. She knew about a small local show that was going to be held near the farm. So, one day after watching Sam ride, Jo said, "Good practice today. How would you like to take CJ to the Patrick Henry Horse Show next weekend?"

The Patrick Henry Horse Show was a small local show nearby. The participants would be other local children similar to Sam and the girls at Brook Hill. Most of them would be beginners or intermediate riders. It was considered a schooling show where people went to learn.

"Are you kidding?" Sam replied excited about the idea.

"You are riding well and I thought it might be a good place to see how CJ does in public with the other horses. Some of the other girls want to go and I thought you might want to go too. It should be a good place to start," answered Jo.

"I would love to go. I have wanted to go to a show for so long! I can't wait to show all my friends my great horse!" Sam said with excitement.

"Not so fast. We don't know how great he will be; that's what we are going to find out," replied Jo. "You have a lot of work to do to get ready. You will have to clean your saddle and bridle, get a riding outfit, clip, bathe, and braid CJ."

Sam and CJ trotted off to the barn to tell the other girls. She took extra care cooling and brushing CJ before putting him back in his stall. Sam and the other girls then cleaned the saddles and bridles with leather cleaner as they talked about the show. There was a hum of excitement in the barn.

The week crawled by; it seemed like a year to Sam! She worked extra hard with CJ and practiced longer every day.

The day before the show, everyone gathered at the barn to make the final preparations. All the girls were getting their horses ready. Sam gave CJ a bath. Jo clipped the hair from inside his ears and around his muzzle. Sam had to stand on a step stool to braid his mane and tail. CJ stood very still as if he knew he was getting ready for something really big.

"You're a handsome man when you are all cleaned up," Jo said patting CJ's neck.

"Mom, do you think he remembers doing this before his races?" asked Sam.

"Probably, but I hope he isn't thinking he is going to a race and run off with you!" laughed Jo.

"Me too," laughed Sam and the other girls.

That night Sam was so excited she couldn't sleep. When Jo came to wake her early in the morning, Sam was already dressed in her black riding boots, tan riding pants and a pretty light pink shirt with a new horse pin clipped on her "ratcatcher," a funny name that the neck ties are called. After putting her hair into a pony tail, Sam grabbed her black velvet riding helmet, and a doughnut off the kitchen table, as she headed out to the barn. The horses finished their grain as the girls loaded the saddles, bridles, and blankets into the truck. Sam carefully wrapped CJ's legs with long red leg wraps before loading so he wouldn't bump and hurt his legs during the trip. CJ, looking very proud, made everyone laugh lifting his legs high as he walked because he didn't like the strange feel of the leg wraps. But, he walked willingly and calmly onto the trailer with the other horses.

"Everyone got a riding helmet?" inquired Jo.

All the girls chimed back with an "OK" as they checked that they had packed all their equipment. Everyone climbed into the pick up truck and off they went.

As they pulled onto the horse show grounds, they saw several of their friends from school. There were many other trailers and lots of horses scattered throughout the field around the show ring. Everyone unloaded their horses. Sarah, Gracie, and the other girls tacked up and rode off quickly to the warm up in the practice ring. Most of them had shown before and knew what to do. Sam became very nervous.

"You're going to be fine," Jo assured her as she patted her daughter's shoulder. "Get CJ tacked up and when you're ready, go warm up in the practice ring with the others," Jo said. Sam put the saddle and bridle on CJ and Jo gave her a leg up. "I'll check on you in a minute," Jo said as she handed Sam her helmet and walked off to enter Sam in a class.

Sam fastened the chin strap on her helmet as they headed for the practice ring. There were boys and girls, horses and ponies, all going around the ring practicing their various gates. Some were trotting in one direction. Others were cantering in the opposite direction. The ring was crowded. Sam was a little worried that all the commotion would get CJ excited. They walked several times around the ring before trotting. CJ was alert and moved quickly. His ears were up but he held his head and neck in a good position, not too high. He was acting good but doing his usual silly stuff. On command, he galloped at a good pace. He shook his head but did not run too fast. CJ cantered calmly and settled in quickly. Sam was feeling confident again.

"How is he doing?" yelled Jo from across the fence.

"He seems fine. He's not bothered by the other horses and is listening well," replied Sam.

"Great, your class is next."

Sam rode over to the main ring just as her class was announced. About 15 other riders entered the ring with

Sam and walked around the rail. Everyone trotted when the announcer asked. As Sam posted up and down, she thought that showing seemed pretty easy. Everything was going well. Sam knew her leads and diagonals so she felt like she was going as good or better than some of the others. Some of the beginner riders took the wrong lead and some didn't get on the correct diagonals when trotting; so Sam felt like she stood a good chance. After walking, trotting, and cantering in the first direction, the contestants were asked to reverse and do the same gates in the opposite direction. After walking and trotting again, the announcer asked for everyone to canter. Some horses passed CJ and he sped up a little.

"It's OK CJ; it's not a race," Sam whispered trying to calm him down.

CJ was galloping pretty fast around the ring and began to pass some of the horses. Sam tensed up a little. Just then a herd of large black cows and calves came up to the fence near the arena. They were watching like a crowd of spectators. But guess what? CJ had apparently never seen a cow before! His head went up, his nostrils flared and his eyes were wide as saucers. Sam was focused on the what she and the other riders were doing and didn't see the cows and didn't know why he was acting like that. She squeezed her legs and pulled on the reins trying to get him to put his head down. Instead, CJ immediately planted all four feet in the dirt and stopped abruptly. He stopped so fast that Sam fell forward and had to grab his neck to keep from falling off. At first, she didn't know what was going on. She kicked and kicked but CJ didn't move. Some of the other riders had to swerve to go around her. One rider had to stop so he didn't run into them and was mad at Sam for cutting him off. Sam didn't mean to cut him off and felt bad about messing him up. She was trying hard to make CJ canter again. Everyone in the class passed by and kept cantering around the ring. Finally, Sam saw the cows too. By this time the class was over. Sam finally got CJ to turn away from the cows and line up with the rest of the horses. Sarah won first and Gracie placed fifth. Sadly, Sam and CJ did not place. Sam was so embarrassed her face was red. She felt like crying and was very mad at CJ as she followed the others out of the ring. When she saw Jo, she jumped off and handed the reins to her mom and threw her helmet on the ground.

"Hold your head up and don't be angry," advised Jo. "You must always be a good sport. This is your first show, and now we know something new about CJ. Who would have thought a horse would be scared of a cow!" Jo said jokingly trying to make Sam feel better. Jo thought it was kind of funny.

Soon Sam was laughing about it too. Then she did something that made Jo very proud. She ran over to congratulate her friends. They all laughed as Sam told what had happened to her.

Sam, like all good riders do, got back on CJ and went back into another class and gave it another try. The rest of the day went better and eventually Sam did win a ribbon. All the girls had a great time. Sarah won the championship and the entire Brook Hill group cheered. At the end of the day, they were all tired. All the girls untacked and walked their horses to cool them down before repacking the trailer and heading back to the farm.

"See you at the next show," called out Sam, waving good-bye to her friends as they drove off.

The girls talked and laughed all the way back to Brook Hill and all the horses got extra hay for a good day's work when they got back to the barn.

Jo and the parents were proud of the girls and how they had done that day. It was a good start to a long show career for CJ and Sam.

Chapter 4

Don't Get Discouraged

F inally, after many months of what seemed like endless practice "on the flat" or riding around the ring without going over jumps, Sam wanted to try something new. Sam had jumped before and wanted to see if CJ's legs and feet could hold up to the stress and strain of jumping. So Sam asked Jo if they could try some simple gymnastic exercises, the horse kind, the beginning exercises that teach horses the basics of jumping.

Jo thought that CJ was fully recouped and agreed to give it a try. She warned Sam that, just like the initial recovery process, she would have to take it slow and just do a little at a time to see how much pressure CJ's legs could withstand, and if CJ showed any signs of lameness after the workouts she would have to give up the idea and settle for showing on the flat.

Sam beamed. She knew that meant she was going to start teaching CJ how to jump. Sam always had confidence in CJ's ability.

Jo began by placing a number of poles, spaced evenly apart, on the ground. Sam would trot CJ over the poles. He looked like he was prancing, picking up his feet so not to hit a pole with his hooves and placing his feet squarely between each pole. This series helped CJ learn the correct strides to take to prepare him to go over a jump. This sounds easy but took a little practice not to hit the poles. After a number of times of trotting over the poles to learn the pacing and being able to execute the ground poles correctly, Jo erected two poles at the end of the ground poles as cross bars which formed a low x shaped jump. Sam would trot CJ over the ground poles and then he was to jump over the cross bars.

At first CJ went through the poles and over the cross bars like a pro. He was athletic and it seemed to come natural. Sam was thrilled. But every time CJ went through the course he got a little faster. CJ became excited and pushy. The more he went through the course the faster he became. He rushed through like a bull in a china shop and hit every pole and knocked the cross bars down. Jo reset the poles. It was up to Sam to correct his strides and his behavior. She would kick him when he hit the poles and pull the reins to collect him and adjust his strides. Over and over Jo reset the poles as Sam circled CJ back to try again. Finally CJ calmed down and went through the pattern without hitting any of the poles or knocking down the cross bars.

Patting CJ's long sweaty neck, Jo asked, "What do you think? Should we call it a day?"

"He's being typical CJ. He'll make a jumper if he would stop being so goofy and playing around, Sam smiled and replied confidently as she swung her leg over and jumped down off CJ.

"If it doesn't kill me first," Jo said jokingly as they walked slowly back to the barn. Jo, Sam, and CJ were hot, dirty, and tired.

Sam was anxious to try again the next day. CJ came out the next day goofy acting as always but showing no signs of lameness. His legs appeared to be getting stronger and he looked fit. But, in addition to being pushy and hard to control through the jumps, Sam thought CJ felt a little flat. He was not rounding his back. So, day after day Jo set up various types of jumping patterns to correct CJ's take off, strides, and landing. After much practice, CJ improved. He became balanced, rounded his back, and folded his knees. He cleared the jumps with grace and ease but Jo noticed something still looked different about CJ's jumping. He didn't knock any poles down but something didn't look quite right. Jo watched for a long time but couldn't figure it out. Finally, one day Jo decided to take some pictures of Sam and CJ as they practiced. It was when Jo looked at the photos that she could see what was wrong. CJ bent his knees under when jumping but he did not bend his ankles. Due to his old race injury, he could not bend his ankles and fold his hooves under like other horses did when they jumped. The feltlock joint had calcified and was more like solid bone rather than a flexible, moveable, joint. This could make it more difficult for him to clear higher jumps without knocking them down. This is something that they could not teach him. He would never be able to bend his fetlocks any more due to his past injury and surgery. But he appeared not to have any problems with the low jumps and looked like he would be a good jumper at this level.

As part of the United Neigh 4-H program, a local horse trainer, Ann, volunteered her time to teach the children at Brook Hill how to ride and jump. Ann was a tall thin blond with long, straight hair. She had grown up showing jumping horses. Ann had worked with Sam for several years with other horses and ponies. Sam, like the other girls at the barn, liked Ann. She was friendly and knowledgeable. She was someone the girls looked up to and wished they could ride as good as she could. Ann saw at once that there was a special bond between Sam and CJ and could tell a difference in Sam when she rode CJ. Both the horse and the rider were making unbelievable progress. Sam had gained much confidence riding CJ. Before long they were not only jumping small cross bars but one to two feet high jumps too. Ann suggested they go to a jumping clinic at a nearby college.

This wasn't a real horse show but a training event that would help prepare Sam and CJ for future competitions. They would be riding with other girls including the college riding students. They would be experiencing new surroundings and new challenges. The advanced riding students and trainers from the college would be giving the lessons. It would be a chance for Sam and CJ to jump new jumps and see how they compared to other riders and jumpers.

The following Saturday was warm and sunny. Several of the girls from the barn, Jo, and Sam loaded up to go to the jump camp. Since it wasn't a show, they didn't braid the horses but they did wrap their legs. It didn't take long to get to the college. The girls talked about their college plans and joked on the way there about being as good as the college girls.

The first lessons were "on the flat". Ten to twenty horses and riders were in the ring at the same time. Everyone had a number on their backs like at a horse show. There were four college girls acting as trainers standing inside the ring. One would call out a gait: walk, trot, canter. As the students rode by, the trainers would call out a student's number and tell the rider what they needed to do to improve. For example, if a rider was on the wrong diagonal, not posting up and down with the correct leg of the horse as they trotted, the trainer would call out, "Number 5, check your diagonal," or "Number 3, you are on the wrong lead." Both things would keep a rider from winning a ribbon in a real show. This was basic and something Sam already knew.

While Sam and CJ walked, trotted, and cantered, everything was going great. The trainers seemed very impressed with Sam's riding. Sam held her hands and legs in the proper positions. Her arms and legs did not move much as she rode. She knew her diagonals and kept her head up. Even though Sam was younger than most of the other riders, Sam was a pretty rider and she stood out in the crowd as being one of the best.

CJ looked very good too. He was a big pretty horse that people noticed. His coat was shiny and he was perky with his ears up. He was moving well and was cooperative obeying Sam's signals. He got his leads right in both directions. He was happy and liked being out as much as Sam.

Then came lesson two: jumping. Each rider took a turn going over the jumps that were set in a pattern around the ring. The instructor would watch each rider go over the jumps and would give instructions as they went through the course. Sam thought the course looked easy. They were to enter the ring, trot a circle, start to canter before heading toward the first jump then jump over the jumps which were set around the ring. There were some cross boards and small jumps similar to the ones they had at home. A number of riders went before Sam and finished the course without any problems. A couple of the horses refused a jump or two, or knocked a pole or two down, but nothing major. When it was Sam's turn, she entered the ring at a walk, trotted a small circle before going into a canter and heading for the first jump. Immediately Sam felt CJ pull on the reins. He began to speed up as he approached the first set of cross rails.

"Slow down!" yelled the trainer.

Sam pulled hard on the reins to get CJ to show down but he didn't respond.

"Slow down!" yelled the trainer louder.

It wasn't that Sam couldn't hear her, CJ was not listening to Sam's signals and he was refusing to slow down. Faster and faster he ran. It seemed like a very short few seconds between the jumps. As they approached the next jump, a box jump with flowers arranged across the top of the jump, Sam leaned up into jumping position and prepared for CJ to jump. All of a sudden, instead of jumping forward, CJ veered to the left, refusing to jump. He slid to a stop and put his head down just to the side of the jump. This was something CJ had not done before and

33

Sam was not expecting it. This threw Sam's body forward and her feet into the air. Sam went flying over CJ's head, hitting the ground pretty hard! The crowd unanimously let out a gasp in fear from what they had seen. CJ ran loose around the ring as the trainer and Jo ran over to check on Sam. Sam landed in the dirt but wasn't hurt, just covered with dust. As Sam sat on the ground, CJ trotted back over and looked down at her. He sniffed her as if he was checking to see if she was OK and wondered what she was doing down there! Sam was not amused and grabbed the reins that were dangling from his neck. As Sam stood up and dusted herself off, Jo asked if she was alright.

"Yes, I am fine," Sam replied hatefully with a red dirty face. She jerked on the reins in disgust at CJ to let him know that he had been bad.

Then came the shocking words from the trainer. She told Jo that she thought CJ was too much horse for Sam to handle. She said she didn't think that CJ was a good horse for any child Sam's age. Sam couldn't believe her ears. This was more upsetting than falling off in front of a bunch of people and her friends! Could this embarrassing moment get any worse?

Then the trainer added, "I think you should get another horse."

This made Sam madder than she already was. Sam's red face now burned with anger. Sam looked at Jo with horror of the thought in her mind. Jo looked in amazement at the trainer. Without a word, Sam and Jo headed back to the trailer.

CJ followed Sam slowly out of the ring. Not a word was spoken all the way back to the trailer. At the trailer

CJ stood close to Sam with his head down as he could tell Sam was sad and upset. He knew he had made a BIG mistake.

"I don't know why he did that," Sam pleaded as she patted CJ's sweaty neck. She loved him even though she was mad at him. "He hasn't ever done that before and I am sure he won't do it again," Sam said hoping Jo wouldn't make her get rid of CJ.

Being very experienced with other jumpers, Jo replied, "Oh, I am sure he will do it again. Almost all horses refuse jumps sometimes. As for being too fast, in the past the only time CJ left home was to go to a race. Away from home, that is all he knows, like everything else, it will take lots of time, training, and patience to teach him differently."

"I know I can ride him and I know he will get better. I don't want another horse. I wasn't ready and it was my fault that I fell off," Sam said tearfully.

Jo was concerned that CJ might have been a bigger project that she had anticipated but she knew Sam was determined and knew the work Sam had put into CJ. Jo had confidence in both of them.

"I know. You are a good rider and I love CJ too. The trainer doesn't know you or CJ like I do. As long as you have patience and stick with him, we will keep trying," Jo replied lovingly as she hugged Sam.

"Now get back up there and go back into the ring and show them that you can do it!"

So even though it scared Jo on the inside, she didn't let Sam know. Jo gave Sam a leg up and Sam climbed back into the saddle and rode back to the practice ring. Jo knew that Sam and CJ needed to work through this problem.

Sam needed the confidence and CJ needed to lean that he had done wrong. Sam was determined to prove the trainer wrong. Sam had learned something from the clinic that day. She knew to always keep her heels down and her legs tight so that she would be prepared and not fall off the next time. Most importantly she also learned not to be discouraged by others. Having faith in yourself and determination will get you a lot further. Riding, like life, isn't always easy and fun. It is hard work and it has bumps. As it turned out, Jo was right, this was not the only time CJ refused a jump. But, it was the last time Sam fell off!

Oxer Jump

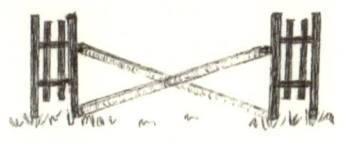

Crossrail Jump

Chapter 5

Never Give Up

Sam was not discouraged about the disappointing and embarrassing mistakes at the first show or the unkind trainer at the college training camp. In fact, both events made her more determined than ever. She had a natural love for, and an uncanny understanding of horses. She was a dedicated and talented rider. Sam was not about to give up on her dream to show and jump. Sam continuously begged Jo to let her go to more horse shows and it wasn't long before they were off to another show.

This time, the results were much better. Sam did get her name called as the winner. In fact, she and CJ won the first of many ribbons. After that, they started going to shows almost every weekend during the summer and her ribbon collection grew quickly. Ribbons began to line the walls of Sam's bedroom. But they were just showing in classes on the flat and in equitation classes which were judged on Sam's riding. Sam wanted to start showing in jumping classes. So, Jo decided to take them to another jumping clinic for more advanced lessons and, hopefully, more positive advice.

This time the jumps were bigger and they were set in a figure eight pattern around the ring. Imagine the number 8 with jumps making the shape of the 8. Starting at the bottom of the ring, the riders would enter the ring and jump the jumps in a curve around the end of the ring. Then they would gallop toward the middle of the ring crossing from the bottom of the ring toward the top of the ring, jumping a jump in the middle of the ring before cutting back to the right. The riders would then jump the jumps curving across the top of the ring and proceeding back across the middle toward the bottom of the ring to complete the figure eight.

It looked like most of the participants were college riding students. Most knew the course and rode through the course fairly cleanly without knocking any rails down. So, with the exception of a few whose horses refused to jump the fences, ie. jumps, everyone stayed on course. Sam warmed up in the practice ring and prayed that CJ would not refuse any jumps. She didn't want any repeats of past fiascoes.

When it was Sam's turn, she and CJ entered the ring confidently and cantered a small circle before jumping the first three jumps. CJ sailed over the jumps with ease but true to form, he got faster and harder to hold. After the third jump, Sam could not make him turn toward the middle of the ring. CJ was out of control again! Sam could not believe what was happening! Her mind raced about what to do. She sat back in her saddle and jerked back and forth on the reins to slow him down and tried to turn him toward the middle jump. But instead of turning toward the middle of the ring, CJ kept running forward and jumped the wrong jumps. It was all Sam could do to keep up with what CJ was doing and prepare herself for the jumps. She felt panicky but had to try to stay composed and think what to do. Now she was worried about how to get him stopped and not fall off at the same time. It all happened so fast she was oblivious to the trainers' voices and noises from the crowd. She was totally focused on trying to control CJ and anticipate his next move and while preparing for the next jump so she wouldn't fall off and make matters worse. CJ jumped all the wrong jumps and kept going around the ring. He ran straight forward without turning toward the middle or stopping. He even jumped the gate leading out of the ring back into the practice area! He was totally out of control. When Sam was finally able to get him stopped, they weren't even in the correct ring! It all happened so fast that the clinic trainers didn't even have time to give her instructions. The clinic trainers stared at each other not believing what they just saw. All the on lookers around the ring laughed. Sam didn't find this latest fiasco very funny. How was she ever going to be able to jump at horse shows if she couldn't stay on course or even in the ring?

Once again, Jo came running over, placed her hand on Sam's leg and looked up at her and asked, "Are you OK? What happened?"

As everyone stared at them, Sam said, "I don't know," shaking her head. "I don't know what else to do but it is time for this goofy behavior to stop!" Sam said angrily as she jerked on the reins to discipline CJ. She was not only mad and angry at CJ, she was frustrated. She was tired of being embarrassed!

Luckily, one of the instructors that day was Mr. Jones. Mr. Jones looked like an old broken down cowboy with old, dirty jeans and worn out boots, but he was a very wise horseman with lots of equine experience. As everyone laughed and Sam pondered what to do next, Mr. Jones moseyed over to Jo and Sam to offer some help. He had ridden and trained horses all his life and had seen horses like CJ before. He took his battered, old, crumpled cowboy hat off his head and politely introduced himself.

"You have your hands full with this one," he said to Jo.

"Do you mean the girl or the horse?" Jo replied jokingly and they both laughed. Sam didn't laugh. She was still mad.

"Well, let's go see if we can't do something with both," replied Mr. Jones.

Mr. Jones grinned a crooked smile and asked if Sam was willing to go work with him in the practice ring. She nodded yes. Sam didn't know Mr Jones but was willing to take any help she could get.

Sam and CJ followed Mr. Jones to the practice ring. Mr Jones knew exactly what to do. First, he changed the bit they were using in CJ's mouth to give Sam more control. He taught Sam how to prepare for CJ's goofy behavior rather than reacting after CJ had pulled one of his stunts. He taught Sam how to use her legs as well as her hands to control CJ's movements. Sam had to push harder with her legs, not just kick with her heels. Sam's legs never hurt so badly but she kept trying. Mr Jones would yell at her to push harder with her legs. So she would push through the pain as she could see the results as CJ was responding. When she would push with her legs, CJ would move away from the pressure of her legs. This helped Sam control him with her legs and well as with the reins. This helped her move him in different directions. They practiced cantering and turning. Sam was able to point CJ in different directions and jump, then turn, and jump again. They could jump circles, figure eights, any direction Mr. Jones told them to go, they went. They also practiced stopping. They stopped before jumps, they stopped after jumps. They jumped two jumps and stopped. They stopped whenever Mr. Jones yelled, "stop." They worked together all day until the sun started to go down and everyone started clearing out. Mr. Jones yelled at Sam a lot that day but at the end of the day, CJ was under control and staying on course. CJ was wringing wet with sweat and so was Sam. Sam had sores on her knees and her legs felt like noodles. Neither horse or rider had ever worked so hard in their life or learned so much. It was the hardest practice day Sam had ever had, but it was also the most fun. It had made CJ a better horse and Sam a better rider. As mean as you might think Mr. Jones sounded, he was actually very patient and understanding. He knew exactly what he was doing. It was his instruction that helped more than anything else they had ever done. Sam loved working with him and he became Sam's favorite trainer and still holds that position in Sam's memories today.

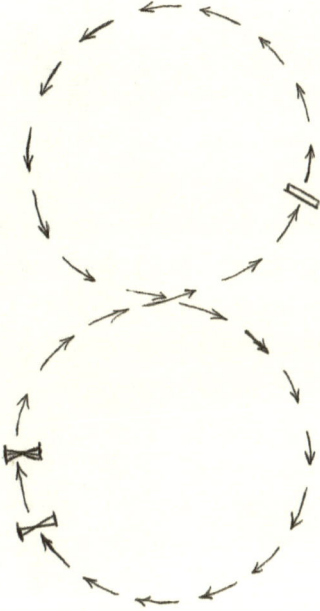

Figure 8 Pattern with Crossrails

Chapter 6

Have Confidence in Yourself

At the next show, Sam showed in the jumping classes. First Sam competed in equitation over fences. This class was judged on her riding style but CJ would have to complete the jumps without mistakes. This course was easy with a few low jumps and cross bars set following the rail around the ring in a circle. One at time time the rider's went through the course. Sam was a pretty rider. Her riding style, leg and hand positions were very good and would stay in position as CJ went over the jumps. Her head was up and always looking in the right direction. She smiled as she rode and looked confident. After all the riders were judged over the jumps, they were asked to come back into the ring and to work on the flat before the final scoring. They walked, trotted, and cantered in both directions. The judge looked to see which riders sat in their saddles with the best posture and least amount of movement in their bodies and legs as their horses went through their gaits. Finally all the riders were asked to line up down the middle of the ring while the judge made her final decision. Everyone waited anxiously for the winners to be announced.

Finally the announcement came, "First place goes to Number 56, Samantha Miller riding Curious George."

Then she showed in the jumping class. This class was judged on how the horse completed the course. Sure enough, the jumps were set in the figure eight pattern. The class was scored according to which horse had the least number of mistakes or faults. If the horse stayed on pattern and did not hit the jumps it was considered as having a clean round. Clean rounds or zero faults obtained the best score. If the horse hit the jumps, knocked the poles off a jump, or refused a jump, it obtained faults. The more faults, the more negative points the rider obtained, the worse the score. If a rider went off course, he was disqualified. The number of faults was announced after each rider completed the course.

Sam warmed up over a few jumps in the practice ring but didn't want CJ to get too tired. Then they walked around outside the ring and watched patiently as the other riders went through the course. Sam was the last to go through the course. She tried to stay focused and confident but she was haunted by the memories of not staying on course. She had to prove that she and CJ could do this. They started over the first three jumps clearing all three with ease. Sam squeezed her legs and pressed him toward the middle of the ring. She could feel him move away from her leg and toward the middle of the ring. They both looked at the center jump. CJ's ears were pointed toward the jump. His tail was flying out behind him. Sam counted his paces and put her heals into CJ and he lifted over the middle jump clearing it without any problems. She pulled to the right and CJ turned toward the jumps across the top half of the course. CJ's pace stayed consistent and he did everything Sam asked. They turned back toward the middle jump. The class breezed by as easy as practice jumping at home. It was over before she knew it. It was a clean round, a perfect score!

The crowd clapped as Sam's name and number was called out first again! Sam could not have been more proud of CJ.

Now that Sam and CJ could compete in jumping classes, Sam had bigger dreams. After two years of showing at small local shows, Sam wanted to go to bigger shows where the competition was tougher. The United Neigh group at Brook Hill formed a team of their best riders and prepared to go to the Commonwealth Games. The girls knew this was going to be more challenging than what they had faced before. This was not a show for beginners. This show was going to be full of experienced riders and good horses. They were going to have to be on the top of their game.

The girls practiced longer and harder preparing their horses and polishing their skills and equipment. They also made special stall decorations to put up at the horse show to display their names and team information. To decorate their stalls, they made banners to hang across the top of the stalls and ordered the same colored blankets showing their team colors. Each girl made a name plaque composed of a collage of pictures of their horses, and a written page telling the stories of their horses coming to Brook Hill which they posted on their stall doors.

Jo and Sam went to Western Ways to buy a brand new outfit just for the show. They purchased a new fitted pin stripped navy blue jacket and light blue shirt. Jo gave her a horseshoe shaped pin to wear as her neck pin for good luck. Sam polished her boots and brushed her black velvet helmet.

The Commonwealth Games was a whole new show experience. It was held at a large show facility in Lexington, VA an hour away. The show would be held over the course of several days so the team would spend the night rather than travel back and forth each day. The team arrived at the show grounds the day before the show started so they could set up their stall decorations and practice in the rings on the grounds so the horses could get use to the new surroundings. The grounds were crowded and horses and riders were everywhere when the team arrived. There were over six hundred stalls and there was a large covered arena and three outside rings. All the rings were packed with people practicing for the show. There were twice as many riders and horses than Sam had ever competed against. There were grooms washing horses in the wash pits and trainers coaching riders over the jumps.

It was intimidating to the girls to see all the expensive horses, fancy horse trailers, grooms, elaborate professional made stall decorations, and personal trainers. The girls were wondering if they fit in. Were these riders better? Were the horses better?

Feeling the tension and nervousness in the girls as they walked around and explored the grounds, Jo said, "We're here to have fun. Don't worry about the others, have confidence. Focus on doing your best and you will be fine. Have fun!" Jo said trying her best to calm the team's nerves.

Just like the girls, their horses seemed to feel the additional tension and were excited too. There were new sights and sounds for them to get use to too. It took a little longer than usual to get CJ to settle down. Sam rode longer than usual that night until CJ was calm and felt like he was ready to show. She knew she would not have time in the morning to prepare him. He needed to be ready to go. Sam was very focused and she had worked very hard to get this far. She didn't want to have any goofy, embarrassing mistakes. The whole team was up late practicing, washing, and braiding their horses. They checked into the hotel late that night, but most of them were too excited and nervous to sleep.

The next day the team was up early and back out to the show grounds before the show began. The grounds buzzed with excitement. Riders were running everywhere frantically trying to get ready on time. If a rider was not at the gate when their class was called, they were not allowed to enter the class. This was a team competition but each girl on the team had a different class in which to participate. Sarah would show in the equitation class, Grace would show in the classes on the flat, and Sam would show in the over fences, jumping, classes. The riders would win individual ribbons for placing in their classes and then the teams would be given medals depending on the total of the team's winnings as compared to the other teams' total points.

The course patterns, the order the riders were suppose to jump over the jumps, were posted prior to the start of the show. The riders were allowed to walk the course prior to the class to learn the pattern and plan their approaches and take offs. It was up to the riders to memorize the pattern so they would not go off course. The jumps were two to three feet high and the course was long. There were higher jumps and a longer pattern than Sam and CJ had ever done before. Jo walked the course with Sam and discussed their strategy.

The show started promptly at 8:00 am. It didn't take any time before Sam's class started but the jumping class was a large class with a long difficult course. Because there were many participants in the class and it took a long time for each jumper to run the course, it took all day to run everyone through the course. Sam and CJ were ready and waiting when their class was called. Jo stood by her side spraying CJ with a little more fly spray and wiping the dust off his hooves and Sam's boots. Sam looked pretty in her new outfit.

Some of the jumpers went off course because they couldn't remember the pattern and were disqualified. Sam watched patiently going over the pattern again and again in her head trying not to get confused by those going in the wrong directions. Many of the horses had faults knocking poles off the jumps as they went through the course. Sam felt better when she saw that not all the riders and horses were as perfect as they looked. Even the expensive horses made mistakes and refused jumps! It felt like they had watched a thousand horses before it was Sam's turn.

When her number was called, Sam patted CJ's neck, "OK boy, let's do this."

"Good luck," Jo said encouragingly.

Sam rode into the ring confidently. They galloped their circle and sailed with ease over the first box fence lined with fake red and white flowers. CJ stayed calm and remained at an even pace. He continued toward the large solid panel box jump lined with cedar trees and cleared it without shying or swerving. He sailed over the easier cross bar jump topped with the green and white pole. Then they turned toward the center of the ring and jumped over the difficult double red and white pole vertical jumps without hitting any of the jumps or knocking off any of the poles. No refusals, no problems so far.

"Good boy, we're half-way done," Sam whispered.

CJ galloped on. Sam's coat tail waved up in the wind as she kicked him forward. But he lifted up a little late coming down short knocking off one pole of the triple oxer. Sam kicked him again and pulled back and forth to collect him and get back on track and ready for the next jump. She gathered her reins and moved her body into point position to prepare herself for the jump. CJ sailed over the parallel jump and finally over the x jump topped with two green poles. No refusals and only one fault. It was a beautiful first round! After clearing the last jump, Sam sighed with relief and realized that she had been holding her breath. Smiling, she leaned forward and stroked CJ's sweaty neck for a job well done. CJ stretched out his neck and slowed to a trot before exiting the ring. Both CJ and Sam were tired from the long hard run. The crowd clapped for a good round. Jo ran over to congratulate her on her performance. Sam jumped off CJ and pulled her stirrups up to walk CJ and cool him off while they waited for the rest of the riders to finish their rounds. Finally the winners were announced. Sam won second place! Proudly Sam walked CJ back into the ring to accept their red ribbon. Jo gave Sam a big hug and everyone patted CJ.

The entire show was very exciting. No one knew for sure how the overall scores were going to come out. The overall team placings were not announced until the end of the show. The girls did not expect to do as well as they did in their individual classes. All the girls on the team placed in their classes which had been unexpected and a wonderful surprise. They had no idea how well they had done overall too. The team finished second overall winning a silver medal! Needless to say they were thrilled! This was a great achievement for the whole team. All the long hard work was paying off. The team celebrated with a huge pizza party and extra hay for the horses. They were all exhausted and slept better that night. They next day they went home with new ribbons and stories to tell their friends and families.

Chapter 7

Dream Big

F ive years had passed quickly. Now Sam had her heart set on making the National riding team. She would have to qualify for the National Team by placing in the top eight at the Pony Club East and West World Games. So plans were made to return to Lexington the next year.

This show was a two day team event with the points being averaged at the end. The teams would compete as before but the top eight riders who earned the most points would be selected to form the National Team and compete at the National Championship Show.

An opening ceremony was held the night before the event. Each team rode into the covered arena and paraded around the ring like the opening ceremony at the Olympics. The teams had matching outfits and carried banners and flags. All the teams and members were announced as they entered the ring. Then there was a big party for all the participants.

Prior to the start of the show the next day, all the horses had to pass an inspection by the judges. This was to assure that all the horses were sound, not lame, and not drugged. The Pony Club is concerned about the care and well being of the horses as well as teaching children how to ride. Every rider had to lead their horse to the judge and trot past the judges. The judges had to pass the horse as being healthy before it was allowed to be shown.

All the participants lined up, and one by one, trotted past the judges. It was a very hot day and the line was very long. It seemed to take hours. Sam and CJ waited patiently for their turn. When it was time for them to go, Sam clicked at CJ and ran beside him as he trotted past the judges. But to Sam's surprise, the judges did not pass her immediately like they had done all the other participants before her. Instead, they huddled together and whispered amoung themselves. Then they asked Sam to return to the back of the line and go again. So Sam and CJ walked to the back of the line to wait. Jo came over and asked Sam what was wrong.

"I don't know," replied Sam. "They didn't tell me," Sam said bewildered.

So they waited together concerned if Sam was going to be allowed to show. Sam and CJ started to sweat while they stood in the hot summer sun waiting to go again. CJ was feeling lazy and hung his head down. Sam swung her arm over CJ's neck and lay against him, tired of standing. Finally their turn came and Sam pulled CJ to trot. He stretched his neck out as Sam pulled, but he didn't trot. He was already tired and didn't want to trot. Jo clapped her hands behind him to perk him up and get him trotting.

Again the judges did not pass CJ. The judges asked Sam to go back and do it again. Now she and CJ were the only ones left; everyone else had been passed and had gone back to the barn to get ready to show. Sam and CJ were getting worn out trotting up and down before the show even started.

The judges crouched down and watched as Sam led CJ by them. It was then that Jo knew what they were looking at and what they couldn't figure out. So she went over to discuss their concerns. Sure enough the judges didn't think CJ moved quit like the other horses but he didn't appear to be limping. Jo had to explain the whole story about CJ's surgery. Finally the judges agreed to pass CJ and let them show.

Sam now had to hurry and get ready for her class because the show was about to begin. All the other girls were ready so they helped prepare CJ ready as Sam changed into her riding outfit. Jo pinned her number on her back and gave her a leg up. It didn't matter if Sam was tired, she knew she had to place in the top eight to make the National Team. She and CJ were going to have to dig deep and give it their best effort. Her first class would be equitation over fences. Sam knew that she usually did well in this class and it should be her easiest class. There were one hundred participants in her class! It took all day to run the class. So after the hurry up to get ready, it turned out to be a long wait. In addition to already being hot and tired, Sam and CJ became exhausted from the wait. The jumps were three feet high and were fairly easy for CJ. He had a beautiful round. He was too tired for any goofy behavior and had a clean round. On the other hand, the class was judged on Sam's riding. Her body was tired and it was hard to hold her arms and legs still. Her responses were slower and she didn't look quite a sharp as she usually did. Sam was disappointed in herself after her round. She knew CJ had done very well but she felt like she had performed terribly. She knew she could do better.

"You are being too hard on yourself," Jo told her trying to comfort her nervous daughter.

It was a long wait to get their scores. Sam came in fifteenth out of one hundred. This was a very good score for the number of people in the class, but it was not in the top eight and therefore, not good enough to make the National Team. Sam would have to score higher in her next class to raise her overall score to make the team. The pressure was on.

The next day Sam rode in "Go As You Please Over Fences." This class is a timed jumping class. The winner is the rider who can complete the jumps in the fastest time with the least number of faults. Faults would add to the time. There was no set pattern but all the jumps had to be jumped at least once. There were timers set at the top of the ring. The time started when the riders crossed in front of the time machine at the beginning of their run and the timers cut off when the riders rode back in front of them after completing all the jumps. The riders could jump the jumps in any order. It was up to the riders to plan their course in the way they thought would create the fastest pattern and produce the fastest time.

Jo and Sam studied the jumps and made a plan and walked the course. This should be a good class for CJ because being fast was generally not a problem, and in fact, was what he did best. But CJ would not only have to canter as fast as he could, he would have to make sharp quick turns and still clear the jumps.

Sam tried not to watch the other participants because everyone had a different pattern and it confused her. She had to remember her plan and not turn in the wrong direction or do anything that would make her pattern longer. Missing a jump would disqualify her. So, she waited in the warm up ring and listened to the times keeping the time to beat in her mind while she rehearsed her pattern in her mind.

The order of the riders had been randomly selected and Sam's number had been drawn early so wasn't long before it was her turn. She entered the ring at a trot and began to canter before crossing in front of the timer. CJ took off like the race horse he was. He headed to the first hedge jump and cleared it with no problem. Kicking her heals to keep him going fast, Sam pointed him to the triple oxer. She wanted to get the hardest jump out of the way before CJ got tired. He lifted and rounded his back beautifully sailing over in style. He switched leads and changed direction instinctively as Sam turned her head and looked at the next jump. They were working together like a perfectly matched pair.

CJ effortlessly executed each jump. Sam had never seen CJ perform better. He was on the top of his game. Jump after jump, CJ seemed to get faster. His speed was like an adrenaline rush for Sam. The more she pushed, the faster he got. Both were having the time of their lives. Their performance was beautiful and exciting to watch. The crowd got louder and louder cheering them on as they cleared jump after jump. Sam did not ask CJ to slow down until they had passed back through the timers. She knew they had done well and listened anxiously for their time. The crowd roared when their time time was announced and they were pronounced as the new leaders! Smiling, Sam patted CJ's neck then waved to the crowd as she exited the ring.

Both CJ and Sam were breathing hard as she dismounted and was hugged by the entire team. Unfortunately the hard part was not over. The hard part was waiting for all the other riders to run. With each rider Sam grew more nervous. Was her time going to remain unbeaten? As the riders went through the course, Sam walked CJ to cool him down and try to calm herself. She had never felt so anxious. She held her breath as each time was announced. It felt like her heart skipped a beat every time the announcement was made. This went on for hours. The times were within seconds of hers.

Finally the last rider entered the ring. It was a tall bay horse. He looked fast and their pattern was similar to Sam's. By this time the riders knew which patterns made the fastest times so it gave them a little advantage. But now it was in the execution. Could they be as fast as CJ? They would also have to have a clean run. Sam stepped on the rail to watch. Even though it only took a few short minuets for the rider to complete the course, it seemed like forever before the rider crossed the finish line and the time was announced. Sam couldn't believe her ears. They had done it! Their time had not been beaten! Sam and CJ had won first place! Sam hugged CJ and kissed his nose. CJ's ears perked up as he knew he had pleased Sam. The team ran over and hugged both Sam and CJ. The crowd gave Sam and CJ another round of applause as they walked back into the ring to accept their blue ribbon.

This was a great win not only because it was a large tough class, but it raised Sam's overall score. At the end of the show, the National Team was announced. Everyone waited quietly to see if their name was called. Number one was called, and it was not Sam. Number two, number three, four, five were called out. Sam was getting very nervous. It was a very close and competitive group. Unknown to Sam, since the riders' scores were so close, and she had scored so low in her first class, she had to get first place to raise her score high enough to make the National Team. Sam had just about given up hope when the last member of the National Team was announced.

"Finally, last but not least, the final member of this year's National Team, is Samantha Miller," was the last thing Sam remembered hearing. It was a dream come true. It was the best day of her life and she gave all the credit to CJ.

Chapter 8

Make Good Decisions

T he National Championships were held in Lexington, Kentucky, not Virginia. It was the furthest away from home Sam had ever traveled for a horse show. The show grounds was at a race track. There were over eight hundred riders from all over the United States. These were the top ranked riders who had all earned the right to compete at this show. In addition to the participants, there were vendors set up in the covered arena selling horse supplies, clothing, and jewelry. It was like a huge convention.

The classes would be the same as Sam had shown in before but the jumps were going to be higher. So in addition to the competition being tougher, the jumps would be more difficult. CJ was use to jumping three foot high jumps. The jumps at this show would be three feet and six inches which would be the highest CJ had ever jumped.

Sam had confidence in CJ's ability and was determined to give it their best try. She had worked very hard to get to this show and it was her last chance as Sam knew she was going to college soon and would not be showing again for a long time. This show was fulfilling Sam's dream and she was going to make the most of it.

Equitation over fences was their first class. This was good for Sam and CJ. Sam was most confident in this class and it gave CJ a chance to practice the jumps. Sam remembered her ride at the Pony Club show and was determined to do better. She did not want a repeat performance and definitely wanted to go out at the top of her game.

As expected, the class was large and long. The jumps were arranged in an unusual pattern which caused the riders to turn the horses more than usual in the jump course. With the turns, the horses would have to change leads, ie. lead with a different leg as they changed direction. Getting the leads correct would increase their score. This was something CJ usually did well and would help Sam in the overall points. The turns were also more difficult for the riders to keep their arms and legs still, held in position, close to their bodies, and look in the direction of the jumps with little movement in their seat.

Sam had new black riding gloves and new diamond horseshoe earrings which showed when she tucked her hair up under her riding helmet. She looked so grown up. She radiated confidence in her perfectly fitted riding coat and tall black riding boots. CJ looked beautiful too. He was dark and shiny. They blacked his hoofs with black polish so they were as shiny as Sam's boots. His braids laid perfectly down his long thin neck and he looked like an elegant gentleman.

Focused and poised, Sam took her turn over the jumps. As they galloped through the course and over the fences they worked in unison like a well oiled machine. They seemed to perform effortlessly, but the course was harder than it looked. Sam and CJ were tired by the time the ended the course but Sam felt very good about the performance. She wasn't sure how she would place because the competition was so tough but she was happy with herself and with CJ. She knew they had done their best, and she was satisfied no matter how she placed.

After hours of waiting and watching, the winners were announced. Sam placed ninth and was very pleased. Sam was a gracious winner. She congratulated other riders on their good rides and the other winners as they picked up their ribbons. Sam thanked everyone who commented on her ride and placing as she and CJ walked back to the stalls. Sam wished to have placed higher but it was a very good placing for this level. She was pleased, and it gave her a sense of fulfillment and encouragement for the rest of the show.

Sam hung her ribbon on her stall as she untacked CJ. She felt like he had worked hard enough for one day and wanted him to feel rested for the jump class the next day. She knew that the jumps would be even harder than the class today.

The next morning, Sam woke up to pouring down rain. She was hoping that the show would be postponed due to the bad weather but, unfortunately, the rain slacked off and the show officials made the decision for the show to continue. But the ground was soaked and muddy. Wet horses and riders in raincoats were seen all over the show grounds. Sam wasn't sure about showing in the slick muddy conditions but she had waited so long for the opportunity, she didn't want to miss it. So she tacked up CJ and went out to the practice ring to warm up. The crowd of riders in the ring made it difficult to practice over the jumps. CJ didn't like the mud splashing up and hitting him when he came down from the jump. He was shaking his head and acting goofy about the mud hitting his face and stomach. He was veering left and right shying away from the puddles and trying not to step in the water. Sam was doing her best to correct his behavior and push him with her legs to force him to run through the mud and water so he would get use to it. Mud covered both of them from head to hoof by the time they returned to the stall.

"What happened to you?" inquired Jo. "Did you fall off?"

"No, but I'm worried about this. We didn't have a good warm up. Please help me get him cleaned up. I have to change my clothes," Sam replied as she jumped down and handed the reins to Jo. Sam picked the mud out of CJ's hooves and off her boots.

"It's no use to worry about him being dirty. He is just going to get muddy again," Jo said as she untacked CJ. She tied him up and let him dry before trying to brush off some of the dirt.

Sam's class was that afternoon so it gave them time to clean up before going back to the ring for their next class. This was a regular jumping class, not timed. It was judged just on the number of faults. The jumps were three feet six inches which was made more difficult due to the mud and puddles around the ring. The ground was also made rougher and rougher as each rider went through the course. Sam was worried as she entered the ring. She wasn't just worried about the jumps being difficult but many of the horses had refused jumps and many of the riders had ended up in the mud. She kicked CJ to a gallop but kept him slow so he wouldn't slip and slide into the fences. But his pace and his strides were off going into the jumps. He was late taking off for the first jump. Sam felt his front feet slide on the landing of the second jump which caused him to knocked off the top rail. Then he hit the top pole of the third jump with his rear hoof as he lifted over the jump. Instead of the pole dropping to the ground, some how CJ caught the pole with his back legs and forced it up between his stomach and his rear legs. He carried the pole in that position for a couple of strides before the pole fell down to the ground tangled up in CJ's legs. This spooked CJ and caused him to be unable to prepare for the next jump. Knowing he could not take the jump, CJ refused the jump sideswiping it. Sam had seconds to make a big decision. All kinds of thoughts ran through her head. Sam still had a chance to place in the class if she tried again and successfully complete the course. But she was worried about CJ. She wasn't sure if the pole had injured him and feared that worse things could happen if he slipped and fell, or slid into a jump. She thought it would be better not to push CJ too hard now and take the risk of getting him hurt. She was disappointed and wanted another ribbon but knew that her best chance for another ribbon would be wait and make sure CJ was in good shape for his best class, the timed jumping. Sam decided to wait and try again tomorrow. So Sam raised her hand signaling to the judge that she was requesting to be dismissed from the class.

As Sam left the ring and rode back to the stall, Jo told her that she thought she had made the correct decision. Jo thought it was best to put CJ's well being before Sam's desire for a ribbon. Before putting CJ up for the day, they cleaned him up and checked him over to make sure he had not been hurt.

"We'll get'em tomorrow," Sam said, patting CJ's neck.

The next day the sun was out again. The day was warmer and the ground had dried out. Sam looked forward to riding in the "Go As You Please Jumping Class" hoping for as good a run as she had at the Pony Club show. She tried not to be over confident in light of yesterday's disastrous go. Jo and Sam studied the jumps and planned the course. Jo walked the course with Sam and discussed their strategy. CJ seemed to be in a much better frame of mind and had a good warm up. Jo wished Sam good luck and watched as she rode into the ring. The crowd was quiet as she cantered past the timer clicking the start of what would be Sam and CJ's last ride; and what a ride it was! True to the race horse he was, CJ thrived on the speed. He looked like a race horse running at high speed from jump to jump. The jumps were tall and difficult for CJ, but CJ had a big heart and gave it all he had. He was truly trying his best for Sam and Sam knew it. She said she felt like CJ was jumping on his own; she just held on and enjoyed the ride.

Their time was good and they held first for a while, but, in the end, their time was beaten. They ended up in third place which was still fantastic for the level of competition. Sam still congratulated the other riders and hugged CJ for a job well done.

Sam and CJ had come a long way and had accomplished a lot in their show career. Sam was thrilled with the ride and how well she had done but was sad to see her horse showing come to an end. She was so thankful to have had the opportunity to do all that she had done and to have had the chance to have such a wonderful horse. Sam posted a picture of her and CJ and her with their ribbon and texted all her friends, "# blessed."

Chapter 9

A Forever Home

Sam and CJ had made many great memories together. Sam will cherish those memories for the rest of her life and she will always love CJ. But it was time for Sam to go to college and she could not take CJ with her. Sam would not be around to take care of or ride CJ any more. She knew that she would have to find someone to take her place. This broke her heart but she knew that the goal of Brook Hill was to find adoptive homes for the horses that were rehabilitated; so she began to look for someone to adopt CJ. Sam wanted someone who would love CJ like she did and would be able to keep him for the rest of his life.

Most of the girls that had shown with Sam were going off to college and the others could not keep a horse. A lot of different children came and went through the United Neigh program at Brook Hill but most of the new children in the program were beginners and were not good enough riders to ride CJ. One fall day shortly after college started, a new girl arrived at Brook Hill Farm. Her name was Rachel. She was attending Randolph Macon, the local college in Lynchburg where Sam had gone to riding clinics. Rachel had ridden all her life and had to sell her horse so she could go to college. She was now a junior in college and missed her horse. She had participated in the Randolph Macon riding program was looking for a horse to ride while she attended college. She was not in the United Neigh program, she was an experienced rider. She had been a 4-H champion with her horse and reserve champion at the regional show at the Randolph Macon Riding School. She was volunteering her time to work with the children and help with the horses. She immediately fell in love with CJ. Since Sam was away, Jo let Rachel ride and care for CJ.

Rachel came to the farm three or four days a week. Even though she was a very good rider, there were things that she did not know about CJ. One day, as they galloped through the fields, a herd of cows came to the fence across the road. Rachel didn't think anything about it. She was enjoying the day and thinking about her weekend plans. But, true to form, CJ stopped dead in his tracks. Rachel was totally unprepared and went flying straight over his head and landed on her bottom on the ground. Luckily she was not hurt and most importantly, she want not mad at CJ. She did not get up and hit CJ or blame CJ for her fall. She sat on the ground and laughed as CJ stood over her and nuzzled her.

"Well old boy, that teaches me for not paying attention," Rachel told CJ as she picked herself up and dusted off her bottom.

When she got back to the barn she told Jo what had happened and Jo told her the story of Sam's first show.

"I guess that makes me the only **other** person CJ has thrown off!" Rachel replied still laughing about the incident.

Rachel became CJ's new companion. She dressed him up as an elephant for the United Neigh Halloween Costume party and she learned how to make CJ do the tricks Sam had taught him. Jo could see a bond between Rachel and CJ but she knew that the decision was ultimately Sam's to make.

Jo allowed Rachel to take him on the hunter pace at the Randolph Macon Riding School. This is a race where the riders follow signs through the fields but do not chase a fox. Rachel and CJ got lost and ran off course in the race, but, because of their fast time, they still placed among the winners.

When Sam came home from college for spring break, everyone had stories to tell her about Rachel and CJ. The stories brought about mixed emotions for Sam. Sam was happy that CJ was being well cared for and was happy, but, she was a little bit jealous that her best friend had a new friend who was taking her place. She was hesitant to meet Rachel because it was hard for her to see someone else with her horse.

The day came when Rachel came to the farm and met Sam. Sam watched Rachel ride CJ. Rachel and Sam had many long talks about CJ and they became friends too. At the end of the day, Rachel asked Sam if she could adopt CJ when she graduated and take CJ home with her. Even though Sam had expected that this was coming and it broke her heart, Sam knew Rachel was the right person for CJ. So Sam agreed to let Rachel take CJ.

Jo continues to check on all the adopted horses to make sure they are cared for until the end of their lives, so they keep in touch with Rachel. Today, Rachel and CJ spend their time riding along the beaches near Rachel's house. Rachel plans to continue to show CJ as long as he is able.

Sam still thinks about CJ almost every day and will never forget him. Sam wants to find another horse after she graduates and plans to go on to jump in Grand Prix jumping events. She hopes that the horse she finds is as good as CJ and has his heart. She will always miss CJ.

About the Author

The author is not a professional writer but a small town girl who grew up showing and loving horses. Lisa knows the hours and hard work it takes to care for and train horses. She became aware of the program at Brook Hill Farm when her niece, Morgan Rogers, the illustrator of the book, participated in the riding program there. The love of horses, dedication, and hours donated by many volunteers sparked an interest and concern that motivated Lisa to transcribe this story in order to spread the word about the programs and service being done at Brook Hill Farm to rescue, rehabilitate, and find homes for horses.